Dog Vaccination Schedule

Dog's name:

_____

Breed:
Gender:
Birthdate:
Weight:
Length:
Vet's Name:
Vet's Contact Info:
Owner's Name:
Owner's Contact Info:
Dog Groomer Contact:

VACCINATION

Vaccine	Immunization Dates				Veterinarian
ARDENOVIRUS-2					
BORDETELLA					
CORONAVIRUS					
DISTEMPER					
HEARTWORM					
HEPATITIS					
LEPTOSPIROSIS					
LYME DISEASE					
PARAINFLUENZA					
PARVOVIRUS					
RABIES					

Notes:

VACCINATION

Vaccine	Immunization Dates				Veterinarian
ARDENOVIRUS-2					
BORDETELLA					
CORONAVIRUS					
DISTEMPER					
HEARTWORM					
HEPATITIS					
LEPTOSPIROSIS					
LYME DISEASE					
PARAINFLUENZA					
PARVOVIRUS					
RABIES					

Notes:

VACCINATION

Vaccine	Immunization Dates				Veterinarian
ARDENOVIRUS-2					
BORDETELLA					
CORONAVIRUS					
DISTEMPER					
HEARTWORM					
HEPATITIS					
LEPTOSPIROSIS					
LYME DISEASE					
PARAINFLUENZA					
PARVOVIRUS					
RABIES					

Notes:

VACCINATION

Vaccine	Immunization Dates				Veterinarian
ARDENOVIRUS-2					
BORDETELLA					
CORONAVIRUS					
DISTEMPER					
HEARTWORM					
HEPATITIS					
LEPTOSPIROSIS					
LYME DISEASE					
PARAINFLUENZA					
PARVOVIRUS					
RABIES					

Notes:

VACCINATION

Vaccine	Immunization Dates				Veterinarian
ARDENOVIRUS-2					
BORDETELLA					
CORONAVIRUS					
DISTEMPER					
HEARTWORM					
HEPATITIS					
LEPTOSPIROSIS					
LYME DISEASE					
PARAINFLUENZA					
PARVOVIRUS					
RABIES					

Notes:

VACCINATION

Vaccine	Immunization Dates				Veterinarian
ARDENOVIRUS-2					
BORDETELLA					
CORONAVIRUS					
DISTEMPER					
HEARTWORM					
HEPATITIS					
LEPTOSPIROSIS					
LYME DISEASE					
PARAINFLUENZA					
PARVOVIRUS					
RABIES					

Notes:

VACCINATION

Vaccine	Immunization Dates				Veterinarian
ARDENOVIRUS-2					
BORDETELLA					
CORONAVIRUS					
DISTEMPER					
HEARTWORM					
HEPATITIS					
LEPTOSPIROSIS					
LYME DISEASE					
PARAINFLUENZA					
PARVOVIRUS					
RABIES					

Notes:

VACCINATION

Vaccine	Immunization Dates				Veterinarian
ARDENOVIRUS-2					
BORDETELLA					
CORONAVIRUS					
DISTEMPER					
HEARTWORM					
HEPATITIS					
LEPTOSPIROSIS					
LYME DISEASE					
PARAINFLUENZA					
PARVOVIRUS					
RABIES					

Notes:

VACCINATION

Vaccine	Immunization Dates				Veterinarian
ARDENOVIRUS-2					
BORDETELLA					
CORONAVIRUS					
DISTEMPER					
HEARTWORM					
HEPATITIS					
LEPTOSPIROSIS					
LYME DISEASE					
PARAINFLUENZA					
PARVOVIRUS					
RABIES					

Notes:

VACCINATION

Vaccine	Immunization Dates				Veterinarian
ARDENOVIRUS-2					
BORDETELLA					
CORONAVIRUS					
DISTEMPER					
HEARTWORM					
HEPATITIS					
LEPTOSPIROSIS					
LYME DISEASE					
PARAINFLUENZA					
PARVOVIRUS					
RABIES					

Notes:

VACCINATION

Vaccine	Immunization Dates				Veterinarian
ARDENOVIRUS-2					
BORDETELLA					
CORONAVIRUS					
DISTEMPER					
HEARTWORM					
HEPATITIS					
LEPTOSPIROSIS					
LYME DISEASE					
PARAINFLUENZA					
PARVOVIRUS					
RABIES					

Notes:

VACCINATION

Vaccine	Immunization Dates				Veterinarian
ARDENOVIRUS-2					
BORDETELLA					
CORONAVIRUS					
DISTEMPER					
HEARTWORM					
HEPATITIS					
LEPTOSPIROSIS					
LYME DISEASE					
PARAINFLUENZA					
PARVOVIRUS					
RABIES					

Notes:

VACCINATION

Vaccine	Immunization Dates				Veterinarian
ARDENOVIRUS-2					
BORDETELLA					
CORONAVIRUS					
DISTEMPER					
HEARTWORM					
HEPATITIS					
LEPTOSPIROSIS					
LYME DISEASE					
PARAINFLUENZA					
PARVOVIRUS					
RABIES					

Notes:

VACCINATION

Vaccine	Immunization Dates				Veterinarian
ARDENOVIRUS-2					
BORDETELLA					
CORONAVIRUS					
DISTEMPER					
HEARTWORM					
HEPATITIS					
LEPTOSPIROSIS					
LYME DISEASE					
PARAINFLUENZA					
PARVOVIRUS					
RABIES					

Notes:

VACCINATION

Vaccine	Immunization Dates				Veterinarian
ARDENOVIRUS-2					
BORDETELLA					
CORONAVIRUS					
DISTEMPER					
HEARTWORM					
HEPATITIS					
LEPTOSPIROSIS					
LYME DISEASE					
PARAINFLUENZA					
PARVOVIRUS					
RABIES					

Notes:

VACCINATION

Vaccine	Immunization Dates				Veterinarian
ARDENOVIRUS-2					
BORDETELLA					
CORONAVIRUS					
DISTEMPER					
HEARTWORM					
HEPATITIS					
LEPTOSPIROSIS					
LYME DISEASE					
PARAINFLUENZA					
PARVOVIRUS					
RABIES					

Notes:

VACCINATION

Vaccine	Immunization Dates				Veterinarian
ARDENOVIRUS-2					
BORDETELLA					
CORONAVIRUS					
DISTEMPER					
HEARTWORM					
HEPATITIS					
LEPTOSPIROSIS					
LYME DISEASE					
PARAINFLUENZA					
PARVOVIRUS					
RABIES					

Notes:

VACCINATION

Vaccine	Immunization Dates				Veterinarian
ARDENOVIRUS-2					
BORDETELLA					
CORONAVIRUS					
DISTEMPER					
HEARTWORM					
HEPATITIS					
LEPTOSPIROSIS					
LYME DISEASE					
PARAINFLUENZA					
PARVOVIRUS					
RABIES					

Notes:

VACCINATION

Vaccine	Immunization Dates				Veterinarian
ARDENOVIRUS-2					
BORDETELLA					
CORONAVIRUS					
DISTEMPER					
HEARTWORM					
HEPATITIS					
LEPTOSPIROSIS					
LYME DISEASE					
PARAINFLUENZA					
PARVOVIRUS					
RABIES					

Notes:

VACCINATION

Vaccine	Immunization Dates				Veterinarian
ARDENOVIRUS-2					
BORDETELLA					
CORONAVIRUS					
DISTEMPER					
HEARTWORM					
HEPATITIS					
LEPTOSPIROSIS					
LYME DISEASE					
PARAINFLUENZA					
PARVOVIRUS					
RABIES					

Notes:

VACCINATION

Vaccine	Immunization Dates				Veterinarian
ARDENOVIRUS-2					
BORDETELLA					
CORONAVIRUS					
DISTEMPER					
HEARTWORM					
HEPATITIS					
LEPTOSPIROSIS					
LYME DISEASE					
PARAINFLUENZA					
PARVOVIRUS					
RABIES					

Notes:

VACCINATION

Vaccine	Immunization Dates				Veterinarian
ARDENOVIRUS-2					
BORDETELLA					
CORONAVIRUS					
DISTEMPER					
HEARTWORM					
HEPATITIS					
LEPTOSPIROSIS					
LYME DISEASE					
PARAINFLUENZA					
PARVOVIRUS					
RABIES					

Notes:

VACCINATION

Vaccine	Immunization Dates				Veterinarian
ARDENOVIRUS-2					
BORDETELLA					
CORONAVIRUS					
DISTEMPER					
HEARTWORM					
HEPATITIS					
LEPTOSPIROSIS					
LYME DISEASE					
PARAINFLUENZA					
PARVOVIRUS					
RABIES					

Notes:

VACCINATION

Vaccine	Immunization Dates				Veterinarian
ARDENOVIRUS-2					
BORDETELLA					
CORONAVIRUS					
DISTEMPER					
HEARTWORM					
HEPATITIS					
LEPTOSPIROSIS					
LYME DISEASE					
PARAINFLUENZA					
PARVOVIRUS					
RABIES					

Notes:

VACCINATION

Vaccine	Immunization Dates				Veterinarian
ARDENOVIRUS-2					
BORDETELLA					
CORONAVIRUS					
DISTEMPER					
HEARTWORM					
HEPATITIS					
LEPTOSPIROSIS					
LYME DISEASE					
PARAINFLUENZA					
PARVOVIRUS					
RABIES					

Notes:

VACCINATION

Vaccine	Immunization Dates				Veterinarian
ARDENOVIRUS-2					
BORDETELLA					
CORONAVIRUS					
DISTEMPER					
HEARTWORM					
HEPATITIS					
LEPTOSPIROSIS					
LYME DISEASE					
PARAINFLUENZA					
PARVOVIRUS					
RABIES					

Notes:

VACCINATION

Vaccine	Immunization Dates				Veterinarian
ARDENOVIRUS-2					
BORDETELLA					
CORONAVIRUS					
DISTEMPER					
HEARTWORM					
HEPATITIS					
LEPTOSPIROSIS					
LYME DISEASE					
PARAINFLUENZA					
PARVOVIRUS					
RABIES					

Notes:

VACCINATION

Vaccine	Immunization Dates				Veterinarian
ARDENOVIRUS-2					
BORDETELLA					
CORONAVIRUS					
DISTEMPER					
HEARTWORM					
HEPATITIS					
LEPTOSPIROSIS					
LYME DISEASE					
PARAINFLUENZA					
PARVOVIRUS					
RABIES					

Notes:

VACCINATION

Vaccine	Immunization Dates				Veterinarian
ARDENOVIRUS-2					
BORDETELLA					
CORONAVIRUS					
DISTEMPER					
HEARTWORM					
HEPATITIS					
LEPTOSPIROSIS					
LYME DISEASE					
PARAINFLUENZA					
PARVOVIRUS					
RABIES					

Notes:

VACCINATION

Vaccine	Immunization Dates				Veterinarian
ARDENOVIRUS-2					
BORDETELLA					
CORONAVIRUS					
DISTEMPER					
HEARTWORM					
HEPATITIS					
LEPTOSPIROSIS					
LYME DISEASE					
PARAINFLUENZA					
PARVOVIRUS					
RABIES					

Notes:

VACCINATION

Vaccine	Immunization Dates				Veterinarian
ARDENOVIRUS-2					
BORDETELLA					
CORONAVIRUS					
DISTEMPER					
HEARTWORM					
HEPATITIS					
LEPTOSPIROSIS					
LYME DISEASE					
PARAINFLUENZA					
PARVOVIRUS					
RABIES					

Notes:

VACCINATION

Vaccine	Immunization Dates				Veterinarian
ARDENOVIRUS-2					
BORDETELLA					
CORONAVIRUS					
DISTEMPER					
HEARTWORM					
HEPATITIS					
LEPTOSPIROSIS					
LYME DISEASE					
PARAINFLUENZA					
PARVOVIRUS					
RABIES					

Notes:

VACCINATION

Vaccine	Immunization Dates				Veterinarian
ARDENOVIRUS-2					
BORDETELLA					
CORONAVIRUS					
DISTEMPER					
HEARTWORM					
HEPATITIS					
LEPTOSPIROSIS					
LYME DISEASE					
PARAINFLUENZA					
PARVOVIRUS					
RABIES					

Notes:

VACCINATION

Vaccine	Immunization Dates				Veterinarian
ARDENOVIRUS-2					
BORDETELLA					
CORONAVIRUS					
DISTEMPER					
HEARTWORM					
HEPATITIS					
LEPTOSPIROSIS					
LYME DISEASE					
PARAINFLUENZA					
PARVOVIRUS					
RABIES					

Notes:

VACCINATION

Vaccine	Immunization Dates				Veterinarian
ARDENOVIRUS-2					
BORDETELLA					
CORONAVIRUS					
DISTEMPER					
HEARTWORM					
HEPATITIS					
LEPTOSPIROSIS					
LYME DISEASE					
PARAINFLUENZA					
PARVOVIRUS					
RABIES					

Notes:

VACCINATION

Vaccine	Immunization Dates				Veterinarian
ARDENOVIRUS-2					
BORDETELLA					
CORONAVIRUS					
DISTEMPER					
HEARTWORM					
HEPATITIS					
LEPTOSPIROSIS					
LYME DISEASE					
PARAINFLUENZA					
PARVOVIRUS					
RABIES					

Notes:

VACCINATION

Vaccine	Immunization Dates				Veterinarian
ARDENOVIRUS-2					
BORDETELLA					
CORONAVIRUS					
DISTEMPER					
HEARTWORM					
HEPATITIS					
LEPTOSPIROSIS					
LYME DISEASE					
PARAINFLUENZA					
PARVOVIRUS					
RABIES					

Notes:

VACCINATION

Vaccine	Immunization Dates				Veterinarian
ARDENOVIRUS-2					
BORDETELLA					
CORONAVIRUS					
DISTEMPER					
HEARTWORM					
HEPATITIS					
LEPTOSPIROSIS					
LYME DISEASE					
PARAINFLUENZA					
PARVOVIRUS					
RABIES					

Notes:

VACCINATION

Vaccine	Immunization Dates				Veterinarian
ARDENOVIRUS-2					
BORDETELLA					
CORONAVIRUS					
DISTEMPER					
HEARTWORM					
HEPATITIS					
LEPTOSPIROSIS					
LYME DISEASE					
PARAINFLUENZA					
PARVOVIRUS					
RABIES					

Notes:

VACCINATION

Vaccine	Immunization Dates				Veterinarian
ARDENOVIRUS-2					
BORDETELLA					
CORONAVIRUS					
DISTEMPER					
HEARTWORM					
HEPATITIS					
LEPTOSPIROSIS					
LYME DISEASE					
PARAINFLUENZA					
PARVOVIRUS					
RABIES					

Notes:

VACCINATION

Vaccine	Immunization Dates				Veterinarian
ARDENOVIRUS-2					
BORDETELLA					
CORONAVIRUS					
DISTEMPER					
HEARTWORM					
HEPATITIS					
LEPTOSPIROSIS					
LYME DISEASE					
PARAINFLUENZA					
PARVOVIRUS					
RABIES					

Notes:

VACCINATION

Vaccine	Immunization Dates				Veterinarian
ARDENOVIRUS-2					
BORDETELLA					
CORONAVIRUS					
DISTEMPER					
HEARTWORM					
HEPATITIS					
LEPTOSPIROSIS					
LYME DISEASE					
PARAINFLUENZA					
PARVOVIRUS					
RABIES					

Notes:

VACCINATION

Vaccine	Immunization Dates				Veterinarian
ARDENOVIRUS-2					
BORDETELLA					
CORONAVIRUS					
DISTEMPER					
HEARTWORM					
HEPATITIS					
LEPTOSPIROSIS					
LYME DISEASE					
PARAINFLUENZA					
PARVOVIRUS					
RABIES					

Notes:

VACCINATION

Vaccine	Immunization Dates				Veterinarian
ARDENOVIRUS-2					
BORDETELLA					
CORONAVIRUS					
DISTEMPER					
HEARTWORM					
HEPATITIS					
LEPTOSPIROSIS					
LYME DISEASE					
PARAINFLUENZA					
PARVOVIRUS					
RABIES					

Notes:

VACCINATION

Vaccine	Immunization Dates				Veterinarian
ARDENOVIRUS-2					
BORDETELLA					
CORONAVIRUS					
DISTEMPER					
HEARTWORM					
HEPATITIS					
LEPTOSPIROSIS					
LYME DISEASE					
PARAINFLUENZA					
PARVOVIRUS					
RABIES					

Notes:

VACCINATION

Vaccine	Immunization Dates				Veterinarian
ARDENOVIRUS-2					
BORDETELLA					
CORONAVIRUS					
DISTEMPER					
HEARTWORM					
HEPATITIS					
LEPTOSPIROSIS					
LYME DISEASE					
PARAINFLUENZA					
PARVOVIRUS					
RABIES					

Notes:

VACCINATION

Vaccine	Immunization Dates				Veterinarian
ARDENOVIRUS-2					
BORDETELLA					
CORONAVIRUS					
DISTEMPER					
HEARTWORM					
HEPATITIS					
LEPTOSPIROSIS					
LYME DISEASE					
PARAINFLUENZA					
PARVOVIRUS					
RABIES					

Notes:

VACCINATION

Vaccine	Immunization Dates				Veterinarian
ARDENOVIRUS-2					
BORDETELLA					
CORONAVIRUS					
DISTEMPER					
HEARTWORM					
HEPATITIS					
LEPTOSPIROSIS					
LYME DISEASE					
PARAINFLUENZA					
PARVOVIRUS					
RABIES					

Notes:

VACCINATION

Vaccine	Immunization Dates				Veterinarian
ARDENOVIRUS-2					
BORDETELLA					
CORONAVIRUS					
DISTEMPER					
HEARTWORM					
HEPATITIS					
LEPTOSPIROSIS					
LYME DISEASE					
PARAINFLUENZA					
PARVOVIRUS					
RABIES					

Notes:

VACCINATION

Vaccine	Immunization Dates				Veterinarian
ARDENOVIRUS-2					
BORDETELLA					
CORONAVIRUS					
DISTEMPER					
HEARTWORM					
HEPATITIS					
LEPTOSPIROSIS					
LYME DISEASE					
PARAINFLUENZA					
PARVOVIRUS					
RABIES					

Notes:

VACCINATION

Vaccine	Immunization Dates				Veterinarian
ARDENOVIRUS-2					
BORDETELLA					
CORONAVIRUS					
DISTEMPER					
HEARTWORM					
HEPATITIS					
LEPTOSPIROSIS					
LYME DISEASE					
PARAINFLUENZA					
PARVOVIRUS					
RABIES					

Notes:

VACCINATION

Vaccine	Immunization Dates				Veterinarian
ARDENOVIRUS-2					
BORDETELLA					
CORONAVIRUS					
DISTEMPER					
HEARTWORM					
HEPATITIS					
LEPTOSPIROSIS					
LYME DISEASE					
PARAINFLUENZA					
PARVOVIRUS					
RABIES					

Notes:

VACCINATION

Vaccine	Immunization Dates				Veterinarian
ARDENOVIRUS-2					
BORDETELLA					
CORONAVIRUS					
DISTEMPER					
HEARTWORM					
HEPATITIS					
LEPTOSPIROSIS					
LYME DISEASE					
PARAINFLUENZA					
PARVOVIRUS					
RABIES					

Notes:

VACCINATION

Vaccine	Immunization Dates				Veterinarian
ARDENOVIRUS-2					
BORDETELLA					
CORONAVIRUS					
DISTEMPER					
HEARTWORM					
HEPATITIS					
LEPTOSPIROSIS					
LYME DISEASE					
PARAINFLUENZA					
PARVOVIRUS					
RABIES					

Notes:

VACCINATION

Vaccine	Immunization Dates				Veterinarian
ARDENOVIRUS-2					
BORDETELLA					
CORONAVIRUS					
DISTEMPER					
HEARTWORM					
HEPATITIS					
LEPTOSPIROSIS					
LYME DISEASE					
PARAINFLUENZA					
PARVOVIRUS					
RABIES					

Notes:

VACCINATION

Vaccine	Immunization Dates				Veterinarian
ARDENOVIRUS-2					
BORDETELLA					
CORONAVIRUS					
DISTEMPER					
HEARTWORM					
HEPATITIS					
LEPTOSPIROSIS					
LYME DISEASE					
PARAINFLUENZA					
PARVOVIRUS					
RABIES					

Notes:

VACCINATION

Vaccine	Immunization Dates				Veterinarian
ARDENOVIRUS-2					
BORDETELLA					
CORONAVIRUS					
DISTEMPER					
HEARTWORM					
HEPATITIS					
LEPTOSPIROSIS					
LYME DISEASE					
PARAINFLUENZA					
PARVOVIRUS					
RABIES					

Notes:

VACCINATION

Vaccine	Immunization Dates				Veterinarian
ARDENOVIRUS-2					
BORDETELLA					
CORONAVIRUS					
DISTEMPER					
HEARTWORM					
HEPATITIS					
LEPTOSPIROSIS					
LYME DISEASE					
PARAINFLUENZA					
PARVOVIRUS					
RABIES					

Notes:

VACCINATION

Vaccine	Immunization Dates				Veterinarian
ARDENOVIRUS-2					
BORDETELLA					
CORONAVIRUS					
DISTEMPER					
HEARTWORM					
HEPATITIS					
LEPTOSPIROSIS					
LYME DISEASE					
PARAINFLUENZA					
PARVOVIRUS					
RABIES					

Notes:

VACCINATION

Vaccine	Immunization Dates				Veterinarian
ARDENOVIRUS-2					
BORDETELLA					
CORONAVIRUS					
DISTEMPER					
HEARTWORM					
HEPATITIS					
LEPTOSPIROSIS					
LYME DISEASE					
PARAINFLUENZA					
PARVOVIRUS					
RABIES					

Notes:

VACCINATION

Vaccine	Immunization Dates				Veterinarian
ARDENOVIRUS-2					
BORDETELLA					
CORONAVIRUS					
DISTEMPER					
HEARTWORM					
HEPATITIS					
LEPTOSPIROSIS					
LYME DISEASE					
PARAINFLUENZA					
PARVOVIRUS					
RABIES					

Notes:

VACCINATION

Vaccine	Immunization Dates				Veterinarian
ARDENOVIRUS-2					
BORDETELLA					
CORONAVIRUS					
DISTEMPER					
HEARTWORM					
HEPATITIS					
LEPTOSPIROSIS					
LYME DISEASE					
PARAINFLUENZA					
PARVOVIRUS					
RABIES					

Notes:

VACCINATION

Vaccine	Immunization Dates				Veterinarian
ARDENOVIRUS-2					
BORDETELLA					
CORONAVIRUS					
DISTEMPER					
HEARTWORM					
HEPATITIS					
LEPTOSPIROSIS					
LYME DISEASE					
PARAINFLUENZA					
PARVOVIRUS					
RABIES					

Notes:

VACCINATION

Vaccine	Immunization Dates				Veterinarian
ARDENOVIRUS-2					
BORDETELLA					
CORONAVIRUS					
DISTEMPER					
HEARTWORM					
HEPATITIS					
LEPTOSPIROSIS					
LYME DISEASE					
PARAINFLUENZA					
PARVOVIRUS					
RABIES					

Notes:

VACCINATION

Vaccine	Immunization Dates				Veterinarian
ARDENOVIRUS-2					
BORDETELLA					
CORONAVIRUS					
DISTEMPER					
HEARTWORM					
HEPATITIS					
LEPTOSPIROSIS					
LYME DISEASE					
PARAINFLUENZA					
PARVOVIRUS					
RABIES					

Notes:

VACCINATION

Vaccine	Immunization Dates				Veterinarian
ARDENOVIRUS-2					
BORDETELLA					
CORONAVIRUS					
DISTEMPER					
HEARTWORM					
HEPATITIS					
LEPTOSPIROSIS					
LYME DISEASE					
PARAINFLUENZA					
PARVOVIRUS					
RABIES					

Notes:

VACCINATION

Vaccine	Immunization Dates				Veterinarian
ARDENOVIRUS-2					
BORDETELLA					
CORONAVIRUS					
DISTEMPER					
HEARTWORM					
HEPATITIS					
LEPTOSPIROSIS					
LYME DISEASE					
PARAINFLUENZA					
PARVOVIRUS					
RABIES					

Notes:

VACCINATION

Vaccine	Immunization Dates				Veterinarian
ARDENOVIRUS-2					
BORDETELLA					
CORONAVIRUS					
DISTEMPER					
HEARTWORM					
HEPATITIS					
LEPTOSPIROSIS					
LYME DISEASE					
PARAINFLUENZA					
PARVOVIRUS					
RABIES					

Notes:

VACCINATION

Vaccine	Immunization Dates				Veterinarian
ARDENOVIRUS-2					
BORDETELLA					
CORONAVIRUS					
DISTEMPER					
HEARTWORM					
HEPATITIS					
LEPTOSPIROSIS					
LYME DISEASE					
PARAINFLUENZA					
PARVOVIRUS					
RABIES					

Notes:

VACCINATION

Vaccine	Immunization Dates				Veterinarian
ARDENOVIRUS-2					
BORDETELLA					
CORONAVIRUS					
DISTEMPER					
HEARTWORM					
HEPATITIS					
LEPTOSPIROSIS					
LYME DISEASE					
PARAINFLUENZA					
PARVOVIRUS					
RABIES					

Notes:

VACCINATION

Vaccine	Immunization Dates				Veterinarian
ARDENOVIRUS-2					
BORDETELLA					
CORONAVIRUS					
DISTEMPER					
HEARTWORM					
HEPATITIS					
LEPTOSPIROSIS					
LYME DISEASE					
PARAINFLUENZA					
PARVOVIRUS					
RABIES					

Notes:

VACCINATION

Vaccine	Immunization Dates				Veterinarian
ARDENOVIRUS-2					
BORDETELLA					
CORONAVIRUS					
DISTEMPER					
HEARTWORM					
HEPATITIS					
LEPTOSPIROSIS					
LYME DISEASE					
PARAINFLUENZA					
PARVOVIRUS					
RABIES					

Notes:

VACCINATION

Vaccine	Immunization Dates				Veterinarian
ARDENOVIRUS-2					
BORDETELLA					
CORONAVIRUS					
DISTEMPER					
HEARTWORM					
HEPATITIS					
LEPTOSPIROSIS					
LYME DISEASE					
PARAINFLUENZA					
PARVOVIRUS					
RABIES					

Notes:

INTERNAL DEWORMING

DATE	PRODUCT USED	NEXT TREATMENT DATE	VET SIGNATURE

INTERNAL DEWORMING

DATE	PRODUCT USED	NEXT TREATMENT DATE	VET SIGNATURE

INTERNAL DEWORMING

DATE	PRODUCT USED	NEXT TREATMENT DATE	VET SIGNATURE

INTERNAL DEWORMING

DATE	PRODUCT USED	NEXT TREATMENT DATE	VET SIGNATURE

INTERNAL DEWORMING

DATE	PRODUCT USED	NEXT TREATMENT DATE	VET SIGNATURE

EXTERNAL DEWORMING

DATE	PRODUCT USED	NEXT TREATMENT DATE	VET SIGNATURE

EXTERNAL DEWORMING

DATE	PRODUCT USED	NEXT TREATMENT DATE	VET SIGNATURE

EXTERNAL DEWORMING

DATE	PRODUCT USED	NEXT TREATMENT DATE	VET SIGNATURE

EXTERNAL DEWORMING

DATE	PRODUCT USED	NEXT TREATMENT DATE	VET SIGNATURE

EXTERNAL DEWORMING

DATE	PRODUCT USED	NEXT TREATMENT DATE	VET SIGNATURE

HORMONAL TREATMENT

DATE	PRODUCT USED	VET SIGNATURE

HORMONAL TREATMENT

DATE	PRODUCT USED	VET SIGNATURE

TREATMENT
AND
SURGERY

TREATMENT
AND
SURGERY

OUR
SPECIAL
MEMORIES

OUR
SPECIAL
MEMORIES

OUR
SPECIAL
MEMORIES

OUR
SPECIAL
MEMORIES

Thank you.

We hope you enjoyed our book.

As a small family company, your feedback is very important to us.

Please let us know how you like our book at:

myra.patton.thome@gmail.com

Made in the USA
Las Vegas, NV
29 October 2024

10716533R00056